12 REASONS TO LOVE THE
BALTIMORE ORIOLES

by Bo Smolka

12 STORY LIBRARY

www.12StoryLibrary.com

12-Story Library is an imprint of Peterson Publishing Company and Press Room Editions.

Produced for 12-Story Library by Red Line Editorial

Photographs ©: Mike Buscher/Cal Sport Media/AP Images, cover, 1; Roberto Borea/AP Images, 4, 28; Denis Paquin/AP Images, 5; AP Images, 7, 13, 17, 18; Bettmann/Corbis, 9, 10, 29; Ron Frehm/AP Images, 15; John Swart/AP Images, 21; Joseph Sohm/Shutterstock Images, 22; Seth Wenig/AP Images, 24; Nick Wass/AP Images, 25; Charlie Riedel/AP Images, 27

ISBN
978-1-63235-208-8 (hardcover)
978-1-63235-235-4 (paperback)
978-1-62143-260-9 (hosted ebook)

Library of Congress Control Number: 2015934313

Printed in the United States of America
Mankato, MN
October, 2015

Go beyond the book. Get free, up-to-date content on this topic at 12StoryLibrary.com.

TABLE OF CONTENTS

Cal Ripken Becomes Baseball's Iron Man 4

Brooks Robinson Cleans Up in the Field 6

O's Pitchers Are Practically Perfect 8

Four Orioles Pitchers Go for 20 10

Pennant Fever Takes Over in Baltimore 12

Earl Weaver Yells and Wins 14

Wild Bill Leads the "Roar from 34" 16

DeCinces Starts "Orioles Magic" 18

Tippy Picks 'Em Off 20

Camden Yards Sets the Standard 22

Jones Is Front and Center 24

Buck Showalter Brings Orioles Back 26

12 Key Dates 28

Glossary 30

For More Information 31

Index 32

About the Author 32

CAL RIPKEN BECOMES BASEBALL'S IRON MAN

Cal Ripken was a 21-year-old rookie when he took the field on May 30, 1982. He was hitting .238 and just trying to make it as a major leaguer. No one had any idea that he was starting one of the most amazing streaks in sports. Ripken played every game the rest of that season. And the next one. And the next one. And 13 more after that.

Teammates came and went. Managers came and went. The Orioles even changed stadiums. But Ripken played on. He played through streaks and slumps. He even played through his share of injuries. He became known as "The Iron Man."

Ripken hit at least 20 home runs 10 years in a row. He was also an excellent fielder. He played most of his career at shortstop. Ripken studied opposing hitters. He learned where they were most likely to hit

Cal Ripken fields a grounder in June 1996 during his 2,215th consecutive game.

Cal Ripken waves to the crowd in 1995 after officially playing in his record 2,131st consecutive game.

the ball. Then he positioned himself to be in the right spot.

Ripken grew up in Aberdeen, Maryland, just a long fly ball from Baltimore. To Orioles fans, he was a hometown hero.

Lou Gehrig of the New York Yankees had played in 2,130 straight games from 1925 to 1939. That record seemed unbreakable. Then along came Ripken. On September 6, 1995, Ripken played in his 2,131st straight game. Ripken hit a home run in the game. He played every game for two more seasons.

"Simply put, I come to the ballpark every day ready to play, wanting to play," Ripken said. "If the manager . . . wants me to play, then I will. That's the way I've always approached it."

2,632
Consecutive games Cal Ripken played.

- Ripken won two American League (AL) Most Valuable Player (MVP) Awards.
- He was selected to play in 19 All-Star Games.
- He won two Gold Glove awards.

ALL IN THE FAMILY

Cal Ripken's brother, Bill, played second base for the Orioles for seven seasons. Cal's father, Cal Sr., spent 37 years in the Orioles organization. He was a minor league player and later a scout and coach. He was the Orioles manager in 1987 and part of 1988.

BROOKS ROBINSON CLEANS UP IN THE FIELD

Third baseman Brooks Robinson bounced on the balls of his feet, his glove ready. The grounder was smashed down the line. Robinson lunged far to his right. He snagged the ball in his glove. Then from behind third base, he heaved a throw across the diamond, right to the first baseman. "Out!" yelled the umpire.

Robinson made play after play like that in his career. He gobbled up so many grounders he became known as "the human vacuum cleaner."

Robinson won 16 Gold Glove awards in his career. That award goes to the best fielder at each position in each league. Through 2014, no other third baseman had won more than 10. There is a statue of Robinson outside the Orioles' stadium. Robinson's glove is painted gold.

Robinson was at his best in the 1970 World Series. The Orioles played the Cincinnati Reds. He batted .429 and hit two home runs. In the field, he made many diving plays. He caught scorching line drives and gobbled up wicked bouncers. The Orioles won the title four games to one. Robinson was named the World Series MVP.

"I played 23 seasons and I never did have five games in a row like I did in that World Series," he said.

18

All-Star Games Brooks Robinson played in during his career.

- Robinson joined the Orioles at age 18.
- He played in Baltimore for 23 years, from 1955 to 1977.
- He won the 1964 AL MVP Award.
- Robinson had a career batting average of .267.

Orioles third baseman Brooks Robinson
makes a diving stop against the New York
Yankees in a 1967 game.

O'S PITCHERS ARE PRACTICALLY PERFECT

The mighty Los Angeles Dodgers were the team to beat in the 1966 World Series. The Dodgers were in the World Series for the third time in four seasons. The Orioles were newcomers in their first World Series. The Dodgers had two future hall of fame pitchers in Don Drysdale and Sandy Koufax. But the Orioles' pitchers stole the show.

The Orioles won the first game 5–2. Then in Game 2, 20-year-old Jim Palmer threw a four-hit shutout. The Orioles won 6–0. In Game 3, Wally Bunker shut out the Dodgers by a score of 1–0. It was Dave McNally's turn in Game 4. He gave up four hits. Frank Robinson's home run was all the Orioles needed. They won 1–0.

The Orioles swept the series, winning four games to none. The Orioles shut out the Dodgers in three straight games. They never trailed in the series. It was one of the most dominant World Series performances ever.

Robinson was named the series MVP. He had four hits, including two home runs. But the story of the series was the Orioles' pitching.

33

Consecutive scoreless innings pitched by the Orioles during the 1966 World Series.

- There were 36 total innings in the World Series.
- The Orioles gave up just two runs and struck out 28.
- The team's earned-run average (ERA) for the series was 0.50.

The Orioles' Jim Palmer winds up to pitch during the 1966 World Series.

FRANK ROBINSON

Pitching won the 1966 World Series for the Orioles, but star outfielder Frank Robinson helped get them there. Before that season, the Orioles traded three players to the Cincinnati Reds for Robinson. In his first season in Baltimore, Robinson won the AL Triple Crown. He led the league in batting average (.316), home runs (49), and runs batted in (122). He was the AL MVP. Robinson played six seasons with the Orioles. They reached the World Series in four of those seasons.

FOUR ORIOLES PITCHERS GO FOR 20

The Orioles' four-headed pitching staff was (from left) Jim Palmer, Dave McNally, Pat Dobson, and Mike Cuellar.

70

Complete games thrown by the Orioles' four main starters in 1971.

- Those four pitchers combined to start 142 of the team's 158 games.
- They combined for 12 shutouts.
- The Orioles' team ERA was 2.99.

THINK ABOUT IT

Pitching puts a lot of strain on the throwing arm. So teams use a rotation of starting pitchers to give each starter time to rest. Four-pitcher rotations were common in 1971. However, MLB teams now use five-pitcher rotations. Why do you think teams made this change? What are some of the positives and negatives of a five-pitcher rotation?

Baseball success begins with good pitching. In 1971, the Orioles pitching staff was the best in the majors. It was also one of the best of all time. Four Orioles starting pitchers won 20 games that season. Only one other Major League Baseball (MLB) team ever did that—the 1920 Chicago White Sox.

Dave McNally led the way with a 21–5 record. Jim Palmer and Mike Cuellar each went 20–9. All three of them had won 20 games for Baltimore the year before as well. Before the 1971 season, the Orioles traded for pitcher Pat Dobson. In his first season with the Orioles, he went 20–8. Led by those arms, the Orioles went 101–57. They won the AL East by 12 games.

Teams in the 2000s use many more pitchers than they did in the 1970s. Relievers play a much larger role. In 1971, Palmer, Cuellar, and Dobson all started at least 37 games. In 2014, no major league pitcher started more than 34. In 2014, there were three 20-game winners in the entire major leagues. In 2013, there was just one. Four 20-game winners on one team? It might never happen again.

PENNANT FEVER TAKES OVER IN BALTIMORE

The 1966 World Series was a sign of things to come in Baltimore. The Orioles won the AL pennant three straight years from 1969 to 1971. They won at least 100 games all three years. That is the only time in team history that has happened.

In 1969, the Orioles won 109 games. They ran away with the AL East title. They beat the runner-up Detroit Tigers by 19 games. Slugging first baseman Boog Powell hit .304 and bashed 37 home runs. But the Orioles were upset in the World Series by the New York Mets.

The next year, Powell was the AL MVP. He hit 35 home runs. He drove in 114 runs. The Orioles won 108 games. They cruised to their second straight AL East title. Pitchers Dave McNally and Mike Cuellar each won 24 games. In the World Series, they rolled past the Cincinnati Reds in five games.

The Orioles were right back in the World Series in 1971. They had four 20-game winners. Frank Robinson hit 28 home runs and drove in 99. But the Orioles lost to the Pittsburgh Pirates in seven games. Still, in the late 1960s and early 1970s, the Orioles were the beasts of the AL East.

18

Consecutive winning seasons for the Orioles from 1968 to 1985.

- The Orioles appeared in five World Series during that time.
- They had five 100-win seasons.
- They averaged 95.3 wins per season, not counting the strike-shortened seasons in 1972 and 1981.

Pitcher Mike Cuellar celebrates with third baseman Brooks Robinson after the Orioles clinched the 1970 World Series title.

EARL WEAVER YELLS AND WINS

Earl Weaver never played in the major leagues. But he knew the game as well as anyone. As Orioles manager, Weaver was the mastermind behind the team's success during the 1960s and 1970s.

Weaver stood just 5-foot-7. But he was a firecracker who packed a lot of fight in that short frame. Weaver's arguments with umpires were legendary. One time, Weaver thought an umpire did not understand a rule. Weaver charged onto the field with a rulebook in his hand. He tore it up and threw the pages all over the field. That earned him one of his 98 ejections.

But Weaver did much more than argue with umpires. He was one of the most successful managers of all time. "The Earl of Baltimore" had a simple recipe for winning: good pitching, good defense, and three-run home runs. Weaver studied past box scores to see how batters had done against certain pitchers. He used that information to set his lineup. Now, that is common practice. But Weaver was among the first to do it.

Weaver also had a keen eye for talent. It was Weaver who moved

1,480
Career wins as a manager for Earl Weaver.

- Weaver managed the Orioles from 1968 to 1982, and again in 1985 and 1986.
- He led the team to five 100-win seasons and four AL pennants.
- They won one World Series under Weaver.
- His overall record was 1,480–1,060.

Cal Ripken from third base to shortstop. Many thought the 6-foot-4 Ripken was too big to be a shortstop. Ripken became a hall of fame shortstop. And Weaver became a hall of fame manager. He was inducted into the National Baseball Hall of Fame in 1996.

Orioles manager Earl Weaver argues with an umpire during a 1985 game against the New York Yankees.

WILD BILL LEADS THE "ROAR FROM 34"

By day, Bill Hagy was a Baltimore cab driver. But in the 1970s and early 1980s, he had another, unofficial job. He was "Wild Bill Hagy," Orioles superfan.

Wild Bill was easy to spot at Memorial Stadium. He had long hair, a beard, and a cowboy hat. He could be found in the upper deck down the right-field line—in Section 34 to be exact. Wild Bill had his own special way of firing up the Orioles' crowd. Waving his hands over his head, Wild Bill would yell to the fans around him, "Are you ready?!" Then, Wild Bill would raise his arms above his head, curving them to spell a letter.

"O!" the fans would holler.

Moving his body into shapes of other letters, Wild Bill would spell out the team name. Fans would yell out the letters as he did so.

"O-R-I-O-L-E-S . . . Orioles!"

Wild Bill's cheer became known as "The Roar from 34."

For big games, Wild Bill even did his cheer on top of the Orioles' dugout.

Wild Bill died in 2007, but he has not been forgotten. The Orioles in 2014 held Wild Bill Hagy Hat Night. Fans got cowboy hats like the one Wild Bill wore.

7
Numbers that the Orioles have retired.

- No. 4 – Earl Weaver
- No. 5 – Brooks Robinson
- No. 8 – Cal Ripken Jr.
- No. 20 – Frank Robinson
- No. 22 – Jim Palmer
- No. 33 – Eddie Murray
- No. 42 – Jackie Robinson (retired by every MLB team)

"Wild Bill Hagy" cheers from the top of the Orioles' dugout during a 1979 game.

DeCINCES STARTS "ORIOLES MAGIC"

The Orioles seemed to have something special brewing in 1979. Then third baseman Doug DeCinces added a touch of magic.

The Orioles had won six in a row when they met the Detroit Tigers on June 22, 1979. The Orioles trailed 5–3 in the bottom of the ninth inning. Ken Singleton drilled a home run to cut the Tigers' lead to 5–4. Eddie Murray singled. With two outs, DeCinces stepped up to the plate.

The Orioles' Doug DeCinces follows through on a swing during the 1979 World Series.

ORIOLES MAGIC VS. "WE ARE FAMILY"

The "Orioles Magic" run of 1979 ended with a trip to the World Series. They faced the Pittsburgh Pirates. The Pirates had their own theme song that year: "We Are Family" by Sister Sledge. The Pirates won the Series in seven games.

DeCinces launched the pitch over the left-field fence. The Orioles had a thrilling 6–5 win.

The next day, more than 45,000 fans flocked to Memorial Stadium to see the streaking Orioles. The team was playing a doubleheader against the Tigers. And there was more magic. The Orioles were losing 6–5 in the ninth inning. Murray crushed a three-run home run for another walk-off win. In the second game of the doubleheader, the Orioles came from behind again to win 6–5. It was their ninth straight win. The Orioles went on to win the AL East by eight games.

After the 1979 season, a song called "Orioles Magic" became very popular. The phrase is still used by Orioles fans. Many trace "Orioles Magic" to DeCinces's game-winning home run in 1979.

102
Wins by the Orioles in 1979.

- They lost only 57 games.
- Nine wins came on walk-off hits.
- Eleven wins came in extra innings.
- Ken Singleton was the team's top hitter with a .295 average, 35 home runs, and 111 runs batted in.

THINK ABOUT IT

After the Orioles had success in 1979, they seemed to keep having success. Do you think that is a coincidence? Or do you think winning makes it easier to keep winning? Explain why or why not.

19

TIPPY PICKS 'EM OFF

Orioles pitcher Tippy Martinez pitched in more than 500 career games. None was quite like the one on August 24, 1983. The Orioles were playing the Toronto Blue Jays. Baltimore rallied to tie the game 3–3 in the bottom of the ninth inning. But by then, Orioles manager Earl Weaver had made a lot of lineup changes. Both Orioles catchers were out of the game. So was the starting third baseman. And the second baseman.

In the 10th inning, backup second baseman Lenn Sakata took over as catcher. Outfielders were playing at second base and third base.

Martinez came in to pitch with a runner on first base. The Blue Jays figured they could steal bases against Sakata. After all, he had not played catcher since he was a kid. But instead of pitching to the next batter, Martinez quickly threw to first base and picked off the runner.

The next batter walked. Martinez picked him off, too. In the Toronto dugout, manager Bobby Cox could not believe it. He told his first base coach: "If anybody gets on, I don't want them an inch off first base!" Willie Upshaw singled. He leaned ever so slightly toward second. Martinez fired a throw to first baseman Eddie Murray. Upshaw was

546
Career appearances for Tippy Martinez.

- He only started two games in his career.
- His career record was 55–42.
- He had 115 saves.
- His career ERA was 3.45.

Tippy Martinez pitches for the Orioles during the 1983 World Series.

picked off, too. Martinez had set a major league record with three pickoffs in one inning.

The strange game had a fitting finish. The light-hitting Sakata, the emergency catcher, hit a walk-off home run.

1983 WORLD SERIES

The Orioles had a new manager in 1983. Joe Altobelli took over for Earl Weaver. The Orioles won 98 games and won the AL East. Cal Ripken was named the AL MVP. His teammate, Eddie Murray, finished second in the MVP voting. Murray hit .306 with 33 home runs. The Orioles faced the Philadelphia Phillies in the World Series. The Orioles won in five games. Catcher Rick Dempsey was the Series MVP.

21

CAMDEN YARDS SETS THE STANDARD

Oriole Park at Camden Yards has been the Orioles' home since 1992. The stadium began a trend that has swept MLB.

In the 1970s and 1980s, a lot of stadiums were shared by football and baseball teams. But a baseball field and a football field have very different shapes. Seats for one sport were often not good for the other. Many of these stadiums were drab, concrete buildings with artificial turf.

Camden Yards changed that. Camden Yards is a baseball-only ballpark. It is made of brick. The field has natural grass. It was built in downtown Baltimore. Fans can visit the nearby aquarium or a restaurant and then walk to the game. There is a view of the Baltimore skyline beyond center field.

Oriole Park at Camden Yards changed how many teams built their ballparks.

1,016

Length in feet (310 m) of the B&O Warehouse beyond the right-field fence at Camden Yards.

- The shortest distance from home plate to the warehouse is 439 feet (134 meters).
- No player has hit the warehouse in a game.
- Ken Griffey Jr. hit the warehouse during the 1993 All-Star Game Home Run Derby.

"It's just a beautiful place to watch a game," said former Orioles infielder Jerry Hairston Jr. "Other places are great, but Camden Yards set the standard."

New downtown stadiums in Cleveland, Pittsburgh, St. Louis, Minneapolis, and elsewhere copied many of the features found in Camden Yards.

The most visible feature at Camden Yards is not actually part of the stadium. Beyond the right field fence is the former warehouse of the B&O Railroad. It is more than 100 years old. When Camden Yards was built, the planners kept the warehouse. It is a part of Baltimore history. Now Camden Yards is, too.

THINK ABOUT IT

If you were building a new stadium, what features would you want to include, and why? Would you want your stadium downtown or somewhere else?

BOOG'S BBQ

During games at Camden Yards, there is often smoke billowing up from beyond the fence in right-center field. The smoke is coming from Boog's BBQ. That is a popular sandwich stand serving barbecued pork and beef. It is owned by former Orioles first baseman Boog Powell. He often can be found signing autographs and talking to fans near the grill.

23

JONES IS FRONT AND CENTER

The ball was crushed. Adam Jones, playing center field, sprinted back toward the fence. He watched the ball. He felt the warning track under his feet. Then, just before reaching the fence, Jones leaped. He reached over the fence and caught the ball.

Then he quickly fired the ball to second base, where a runner was tagged out.

Jones had taken away a home run and started a remarkable double play. Plays like that show why Jones has been an All-Star and Gold Glove-winning outfielder.

Before Jones came to Baltimore, the Orioles had suffered through 10 straight losing seasons. Jones soon helped put an end to that. The Orioles got Jones in a trade with the Seattle Mariners. He was just 22 when the Orioles traded for him. He had not yet played a full major league season. But the Orioles saw

Orioles center fielder Adam Jones follows through on a three-run home run during a 2013 game.

3

Consecutive Gold Glove awards won by Adam Jones from 2012 to 2014.

- Jones also won a Gold Glove in 2009.
- Paul Blair won eight Gold Gloves, the most by an Orioles outfielder.
- Blair played for the Orioles from 1964 to 1976.

THE PIE MAN

Adam Jones has started his own tradition in Baltimore. After a big Orioles win, he will sneak up behind a player being interviewed on television and shove a shaving cream "pie" in his face. The fans roar when they see Jones with a pie in his hand. After the Orioles clinched a playoff spot in 2014, Jones celebrated with fans by shoving pies in some of their faces.

a future star. Jones was an All-Star in his second year with the team. Between 2011 and 2014, he hit at least 25 home runs every year. His defense was among the best in baseball.

Jones led the Orioles to the playoffs in 2012. Two years later, they won the AL East for the first time in 17 years. Front and center in the Orioles' return to the top was Adam Jones.

Jones makes a diving catch during a 2008 game.

BUCK SHOWALTER BRINGS ORIOLES BACK

The Orioles had fallen on hard times in the early 2000s. After trips to the playoffs in 1996 and 1997, the team suffered through 14 straight losing seasons. Losing 90 games in a season was common. Then along came Buck Showalter.

Showalter was like a doctor to ailing baseball teams. He nursed them back to health. He did that in New York, Arizona, and Texas.

Showalter was the Arizona Diamondbacks' manager in the late 1990s. His first Diamondbacks team won 65 games. The next year they won 100. In 2003, Showalter took over the Texas Rangers. They won 71 games in his first year. The next year, they won 89.

Showalter became the Orioles manager in the middle of the 2010 season. It was another rescue mission. In Showalter's first full season, the Orioles lost 93 games. But once again, he had the winning touch. The next year, they won 93. They made the playoffs as a wild-card team.

In 2014, Showalter and the Orioles did even better. All-Star catcher Matt Wieters and third baseman Manny Machado missed much of

3
AL Manager of the Year Awards Buck Showalter has won.

- He won in 1994 with the New York Yankees.
- He won in 2004 with the Texas Rangers.
- He won in 2014 with the Orioles.

Orioles manager Buck Showalter gives direction to his players during the 2014 playoffs.

the season with injuries. But Showalter got the most out of the players who filled in. The Orioles won the AL East with a record of 96–66. Showalter had done it again.

12 KEY DATES

1902

After one year in Milwaukee, the Brewers move to St. Louis and are renamed the Browns.

1944

The Browns make their only World Series during their time in St. Louis but lose in six games to the crosstown St. Louis Cardinals.

1954

The team moves from St. Louis to Baltimore and changes its name to the Orioles.

1966

The Orioles dominate the powerful Los Angeles Dodgers in the World Series. Baltimore never trails while sweeping the series in four games.

1968

Earl Weaver takes over as manager of the Orioles. Over 17 seasons, he leads the team to 1,480 wins, four pennants, and one World Series title—and also has 98 ejections.

1970

Orioles third baseman Brooks Robinson wins the World Series MVP Award as Baltimore beats the Cincinnati Reds in five games. Robinson hits .429 with two home runs while playing spectacularly in the field.

1971
Four Orioles starting pitchers—Dave McNally, Jim Palmer, Mike Cuellar, and Pat Dobson—each win 20 games and the Orioles run away with the AL East title.

1983
The Orioles beat the Philadelphia Phillies in five games to win a third World Series.

1992
The Orioles move to Oriole Park at Camden Yards in downtown Baltimore.

1995
Orioles shortstop Cal Ripken plays in his 2,131st consecutive game, breaking Lou Gehrig's record.

2010
In the midst of 14 straight losing seasons, the Orioles hire Buck Showalter as manager. In 2012, he leads the team to 93 wins and a playoff berth.

2014
The Orioles win their division and then reach the AL Championship Series for the first time since 1997.

GLOSSARY

box score
A listing of a baseball game featuring key individual and team statistics.

ejection
The act of being removed from a game, often because of poor conduct. An ejected player or manager is not allowed to stay in the dugout, either.

pennant
A league championship.

pickoff
When a pitcher, instead of throwing a pitch, throws to a base, where a teammate tags out an opposing runner.

rookie
A player in his first year in a league.

scout
A person who watches and evaluates players and teams.

strike
When workers refuse to do their jobs as a protest.

Triple Crown
In baseball, leading the league in batting average, home runs, and runs batted in.

walk-off
When the team at bat scores the winning run in the last inning to end the game immediately.

warning track
A wide strip of dirt that runs near the outfield fence. A fielder looking up at a ball knows he is near the wall when he feels the warning track under his feet.

wild-card
Playoff spots that go to the best teams that did not win their divisions.

FOR MORE INFORMATION

Books

Berney, Louis. *Tales from the Baltimore Orioles Dugout.* New York: Sports
Publishing, 2012.

Eisenberg, John. *From 33rd Street to Camden Yards: An Oral History of the
Baltimore Orioles.* New York: Contemporary Books, 2001.

Loverro, Thom. *Orioles Essential.* Chicago: Triumph Books, 2007.

Websites

Baltimore Orioles
www.orioles.com

Baseball Hall of Fame
www.baseballhall.org

Baseball-Reference
www.baseball-reference.com

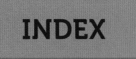

INDEX

Altobelli, Joe, 21
Arizona Diamondbacks, 26

Bunker, Wally, 8

Camden Yards, 22–23
Cincinnati Reds, 6, 9, 12
Cuellar, Mike, 11, 12

DeCinces, Doug, 18–19
Dempsey, Rick, 21
Detroit Tigers, 12, 18–19
Dobson, Pat, 11

Hagy, Bill, 16
Hairston, Jerry, Jr., 23

Jones, Adam, 24–25

Los Angeles Dodgers, 8

Machado, Manny, 26
Martinez, Tippy, 20–21
McNally, Dave, 8, 11, 12
Memorial Stadium, 16, 19
Murray, Eddie, 18, 19, 20, 21

New York Mets, 12
New York Yankees, 5

"Orioles Magic," 19

Palmer, Jim, 8, 11
Philadelphia Phillies, 21
Pittsburgh Pirates, 12, 19
Powell, Boog, 12, 23

Ripken, Cal, 4–5, 15, 21
Robinson, Brooks, 6
Robinson, Frank, 8, 9, 12

Sakata, Lenn, 20–21
Seattle Mariners, 24
Showalter, Buck, 26–27
Singleton, Ken, 18

Texas Rangers, 26
Toronto Blue Jays, 20

Weaver, Earl, 14–15, 20, 21
Wieters, Matt, 26
World Series, 6, 8, 9, 12, 19, 21

About the Author

Bo Smolka is a former sports copyeditor at the *Baltimore Sun* and former sports information director at Bucknell University, his alma mater. He grew up in Washington DC but spent many summer nights going to Orioles games at Memorial Stadium. He lives in Baltimore with his wife and two children.

READ MORE FROM 12-STORY LIBRARY

Every 12-Story Library book is available in many formats, including Amazon Kindle and Apple iBooks. For more information, visit your device's store or 12StoryLibrary.com.